A Picture Book of Sacagawea

David A. Adler • illustrated by Dan Brown

Holiday House / New York

The author and illustrator would like to thank
Brigham D. Madsen,
Emeritus Professor of History,
University of Utah,
for his help.

Library of Congress Cataloging-in-Publication Data
Adler, David A.
A picture book of Sacagawea/David A. Adler; illustrated by Dan Brown.—1st ed.
p. cm.—(Picture book biography)
Summary: A biography of the Shoshone woman
who joined the Lewis and Clark Expedition.
ISBN: 0-8234-1485-X
1. Sacagawea, 1786–1884 Juvenile literature. 2. Sacagawea, 1786–1884 Pictorial works
Juvenile literature. 3. Shoshoni women Biography Juvenile literature.
4. Shoshoni Indians Biography Juvenile literature.
5. Lewis and Clark Expedition (1804–1806)—Juvenile literature. [1. Sacagawea, 1786–1884.
2. Shoshoni Indians Biography. 3. Indians of North America Biography.
4. Women Biography. 5. Lewis and Clark Expedition (1804–1806).]
I. Brown, Dan 1949–   ill. II. Title.
III. Series: Adler, David A. Picture book biography.
F592.7.S123A3 2000
978.004′9745′0092—dc21
99–37135
{B}   CIP

ISBN 0-8234-1665-8 (pbk.)

For Eve Feldman,
colleague and friend
D. A. A.

For Betty,
my wife, my agent,
my inspiration.
D. B.

Sacagawea was born in 1788 or 1789 in the western Rocky Mountains. She was a Native American, a Shoshone.

The Shoshone lived in tepees. They moved to gather food as the seasons changed. They ate seeds, berries, roots, and insects. In the spring and summer they fished, and in the fall they hunted bison. The Shoshone hunted jackrabbits, antelope, and other animals, too. They used branches to make beautiful baskets, bowls, hats, and traps.

The Shoshone were a peaceful people. But they were surrounded by enemy tribes. When Sacagawea was either ten or eleven, a large Hidatsa war party attacked. They stole Shoshone horses and killed many men, women, and children, including Sacagawea's mother.

Sacagawea ran.

She was caught by a Hidatsa warrior and taken prisoner. The Hidatsa took her hundreds of miles away to their village near where the Knife and Missouri Rivers cross.

The Hidatsa were taller and lighter skinned than the Shoshone. They spoke a different language, too. The Hidatsa didn't move around to gather food. Instead, they planted corn, beans, squash, sunflowers, and tobacco. They lived in large, round, earthen houses, made pottery, and built boats for travel on the Missouri River.

Sacagawea worked in the fields. She also helped dry the vegetables and store them for the winter. Sacagawea lived and worked among the Hidatsa, but she was still their captive.

After a few years, the Hidatsa sold Sacagawea to Toussaint Charbonneau, a white trader and trapper. Charbonneau was in his forties. He was a rough, loud man. He had a wife and son. He bought Sacagawea to be his second wife.

In 1804 two white explorers, Captains Meriwether Lewis and William Clark, and their Corps of Discovery of some forty soldiers, frontiersmen, and boatmen, were sent by President Thomas Jefferson to explore the Missouri River and find a route to the Pacific Ocean. They were to draw maps, discover new plants and animals, and learn about the Native Americans who lived in the West, telling them about the United States. On their way up the river the Corps encountered several Native American tribes, including the Yankton Sioux, the Teton Sioux, and the Arikaras.

Soon after Sacagawea was sold, the Corps arrived at the Hidatsa village where she lived.

Lewis and Clark's arrival stirred quite a bit of attention.

The Hidatsa had never seen a flat-bottomed keelboat like the one the explorers traveled in, nor heard violin music. But York, Captain Clark's slave, was their greatest surprise. He was the first black man they had ever seen.

Lewis and Clark met with the local chiefs. Then they and their men prepared for the winter. They cut down trees and built a fort, Fort Mandan, with eight small log cabins inside.

Charbonneau went with Sacagawea to meet with Lewis and Clark. He gave them bison-skin robes and said he could help them. While he couldn't speak all the languages of the different tribes Lewis and Clark would meet, he could talk to them using sign language.

Charbonneau was hired as an interpreter. Because the group would pass through Shoshone territory, Sacagawea would accompany them.

Charbonneau and Sacagawea stayed in Fort Mandan with the explorers through the very cold winter.

Sacagawea was pregnant. In February 1805 her son, Jean Baptiste, was born.

By early April, the frozen Missouri River began to melt. The explorers saw geese flying north. They sent the keelboat and some men back to St. Louis with reports for President Jefferson and nine boxes of animal skins, plants, stuffed birds and snakes. They also sent a pair of elk horns and cages carrying a live squirrel, a hen, and four magpies. Lewis and Clark and their "Corps of Discovery" began their trip west.

Sacagawea was the only woman along. She traveled with her baby in a cradleboard tied to her back. At two months old, Jean Baptiste was the youngest member of the group.

From the beginning, Sacagawea was an important member of the Lewis and Clark Expedition. On the second day out, she collected edible roots for the men. Later she gathered wild strawberries, plums, gooseberries, and currants.

On May 14 a gust of wind pushed one of the explorers' boats onto its side. Charbonneau panicked and dropped the rudder. The boat filled with water. While the men struggled to save the boat, Sacagawea saved the instruments and medicines that had fallen overboard.

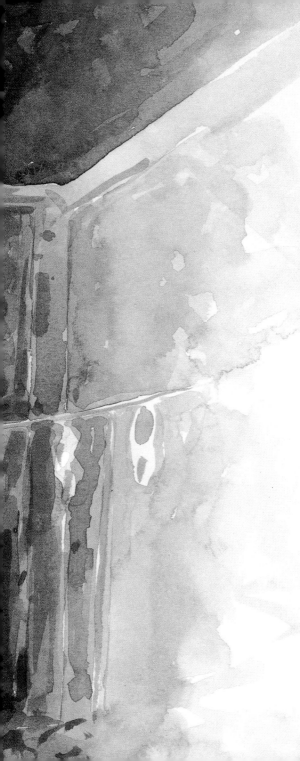

On August 12 the group crossed the Continental Divide, the line of high land that separates the rivers flowing east to the Atlantic from those flowing west to the Pacific. The next day, they met Sacagawea's people, the Shoshone. Captain Clark wrote in his journal that on seeing them, Sacagawea "danced for the joyful sight."

Captains Lewis and Clark met in a tent with the Shoshone leader, Chief Cameahwait. They smoked a peace pipe together and then sent for Sacagawea, who spoke Shoshone.

Sacagawea began to interpret. Then she looked at the chief and jumped up. She ran to the chief, hugged him, and cried.

Chief Cameahwait was Sacagawea's brother.

With Sacagawea's help, the Shoshone traded a number of horses to the explorers. They also gave them a guide, who helped them west through the Bitterroot Range of the Rocky Mountains.

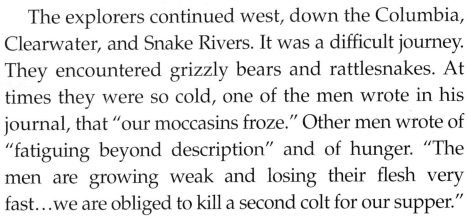

The explorers continued west, down the Columbia, Clearwater, and Snake Rivers. It was a difficult journey. They encountered grizzly bears and rattlesnakes. At times they were so cold, one of the men wrote in his journal, that "our moccasins froze." Other men wrote of "fatiguing beyond description" and of hunger. "The men are growing weak and losing their flesh very fast…we are obliged to kill a second colt for our supper."

Along the way, the explorers met many other tribes. Clark wrote in his journal that seeing Sacagawea convinced "these people of our friendly intentions," because among them "no woman ever accompanied a war party." And surely not a woman with her baby.

In early November the Corps saw sea otters swimming in the river and knew they were getting close to the Pacific Ocean. Then they heard the roar of the waves, and Captain Clark wrote in his journal, "Ocean in view! O! The joy!"

For Sacagawea, seeing what she called "the great waters" and the remains of a beached whale, which she called a "monstrous fish," were highlights of the trip.

It was late in the year. Snow and ice blocked their way back, so, at the edge of the Pacific Ocean, they built Fort Clatsop. They stayed there through a difficult winter of almost constant rain and cold, until March 23, 1806, when they began their journey home.

In August the explorers reached Fort Mandan. This was the end of the journey for Sacagawea, Charbonneau, and Jean Baptiste.

In September Captains Lewis and Clark reached St. Louis. They brought back maps and information about the geography, animals, and resources of the region. They also had made peaceful contact with many Native American tribes.

In a December 1806 message to Congress, President Jefferson wrote that the Lewis and Clark Expedition "has had all the success which could have been expected.... Lewis and Clark, and their brave companions, have by this arduous service deserved well of their country."

Little is known of Sacagawea after the Expedition. Some historians believe that she died of a "putrid fever" some years later, on December 20, 1812. Others say she returned to the Shoshone people and died among them more than seventy years later, on April 9, 1884. But whatever her later history, during her seventeen months as part of the Lewis and Clark Expedition, she helped assure the success of the journey and open up the continent to the people of the United States.

A river in Montana, lakes in Washington and North Dakota, and mountains in Montana, Wyoming, Oregon, and Idaho have been named for her. There are numerous statues and markers across the United States and now a dollar coin to honor her.

IMPORTANT DATES

1788 or 1789	Born in western Rocky Mountains in present-day Idaho
1799	Captured by Hidatsa and given the name Sacagawea, which means "Bird Woman"
1803	The United States purchased the Louisiana Territory from France
May 14, 1804	Lewis and Clark began their journey of discovery from Camp Dubois near St. Louis, Missouri
November 1804	Sacagawea, along with her husband, joined Lewis and Clark and the Corps of Discovery at the newly built Fort Mandan
February 1805	Son Jean Baptiste was born
April 7, 1805	Expedition left Fort Mandan
October 16, 1805	Expedition reached Columbia River
November 1805	Expedition reached Pacific Ocean
August 1806	Expedition returned to Fort Mandan

Sacagawea died either December 20, 1812, or April 9, 1884.

AUTHOR'S NOTE

Sacagawea's birthplace is in present-day Idaho. The Hidatsa village was in today's North Dakota.

When Sacagawea was with the Shoshone, it is believed her name was "HeToe" or "Huichu," which means "Little Bird."

The Hidatsa are also known as the Minnetaree.

According to some sources, Charbonneau didn't buy Sacagawea. He won her in a game of chance.

Captain Clark gave York his freedom soon after the return of the Expedition.

Jean Baptiste Charbonneau, Sacagawea's son and the youngest member of the Expedition, later became a fur trader and an explorer. He spent some time at Bent's Fort in Colorado and was described in a journal kept there as "the best man on foot on the plains or in the Rocky Mountains." In the mid 1840s, he traveled to California, where he settled and remained until 1866. In the spring of that year, he headed to the goldfields of Montana, when he became ill and died.

SELECTED BIBLIOGRAPHY

Brown, Dee. *The Westerners*. New York: Holt, Rinehart and Winston, 1974.

Clark, Ella E. and Margot Edmonds. *Sacagawea of the Lewis and Clark Expedition*. Berkeley: University of California Press, 1979.

Duncan, Dayton. *Lewis and Clark: An Illustrated History*. New York: Alfred A. Knopf, 1997.

Howard, Harold P. *Sacajawea*. Norman, Okla.: University of Oklahoma Press, 1987.

Rowland, Della. *The Story of Sacajawea: Guide to Lewis and Clark*. Milwaukee: Gareth Stevens Publishing, 1989.

Spencer, Robert F. and Jesse D. Jennings, et al. *The Native Americans: Ethnology and the Background of the North American Indians*. New York: Harper & Row, 1977.

White, Alana J. *Sacagawea: Westward with Lewis and Clark*. Springfield, New Jersey: Enslow, 1997.